Presented to:

Naomi Hosselman

By:

Date:

Occasion:

Being the Person God Made You to Be
ISBN 1-57794-445-3
Copyright © 2001 by Joyce Meyer
Life In The Word, Inc.
P. O. Box 655
Fenton, Missouri 63026

Published by Harrison House, Inc.
P. O. Box 35035
Tulsa, Oklahoma 74153

Discover the Joy of

BEING THE PERSON GOD MADE YOU TO BE

JOYCE MEYER

Harrison House

Contents

Part One:
SELF-ACCEPTANCE 9

The Root of Rejection 11
Godly Self-Love 13
The Dead-Dog Image 15
Are You a Grasshopper? 17
God Has a Plan 19
It's Your Choice! 21
Self-Acceptance Allows Change 23
"How Can I Change?" 25

Part Two:
HEALING FOR DAMAGED EMOTIONS 29

One Step at a Time 31
Jesus and Emotions 33
No Pain, No Gain! 35
Do You Want to Get Well? 37
Face the Truth 39
Obey the Word 41
Confess Your Faults 43
Receive Forgiveness and Forget Your Sin 45

Part Three:
CONFIDENCE 49

Get Rid of the Failure Syndrome 51
The Lie About Self-Confidence 53
Have Confidence in God Alone 55
Be Consistently Confident 57
More Than Conquerors 59
The Torment of Self-Doubt 61
Confident to Be Different 63
Don't Lose Yourself 65

Part Four:
DEVELOP YOUR POTENTIAL — 69

Don't Make Small Plans — 71
Draw Upon the Strength of the Lord — 73
Running the Race — 75
Be Temperate in All Things — 77
God's Way Is Better — 79
Wait on God's Perfect Timing — 81
Begun by Faith, Finished by Faith — 83
From Glory to Glory — 85

Part Five:
EXPERIENCING THE LOVE OF GOD — 89

Love, Trust, and Faith — 91
God's Love Will Change You — 93
Love Is Unconditional — 95
God's Love Overcomes and Transforms — 97
Love Never Fails — 99
Believe and Receive God's Love — 101
Understand God's Love — 103
Let Love Take Charge — 105

Part Six:
LOVING OTHERS — 109

Take the Pressure Off Other People — 111
Loving With Material Goods — 113
Everyone Needs a Blessing — 115
Love Gives Preference to Others — 117
Love Is Impartial — 119
Free to Be Servants — 121
Don't Let Selfishness Win the War — 123
Develop the Habit of Love — 125

SELF-
ACCEPTANCE

*You will never sense fulfillment in life
unless you reach the goal of being
yourself. Don't be in competition
with others; just concentrate on
fulfilling your potential.*

GOD'S WORD FOR YOU

May Christ through your faith [actually] dwell (settle down, abide, make His permanent home) in your hearts! May you be rooted deep in love and founded securely on love.

EPHESIANS 3:17

one

SELF-ACCEPTANCE

During my years of ministry, I have discovered that most people really don't like themselves. This is a very big problem, much bigger than one might think initially. It is certainly not God's will for His children to feel this way. Rather, it is a part of Satan's attempt to ruin us.

If we don't get along with ourselves, we won't get along with other people. When we reject ourselves, it may seem to us that others reject us as well. Relationships are a vital part of our lives. How we feel about ourselves is a determining factor in our success in life and in relationships.

Our self-image is the inner picture we carry of ourselves. If what we see is not healthy, not true to the Scriptures, we will suffer from fear, insecurity, and various misconceptions about ourselves. For many years, it devastated my own life.

God is a God of hearts. He sees our heart, not just the exterior shell we live in (the flesh) that seems to get us into so much trouble. Our Father in heaven never intended for us to feel bad about ourselves. He wants us to know ourselves and yet accept ourselves in the same way that He does.

Jesus came to bring restoration to our lives.
One of the things He came to restore
is a healthy, balanced self-image.

GOD'S WORD FOR YOU

And God saw everything that He had made, and behold, it was very good (suitable, pleasant) and He approved it completely. And there was evening and there was morning, a sixth day.

GENESIS 1:31

THE ROOT OF REJECTION

Rejection starts as a seed that is planted in our lives through different things that happen to us. The devil does not want to plant just a seed of rejection. He wants to plant it deep so it will develop into a root that will go way down and have other little rootlets attached to it. Eventually these roots and rootlets will become a tree.

Whatever you are rooted in will determine the fruit in your life—good or bad. If you are rooted in rejection, abuse, shame, guilt, or a poor self-image —if you are rooted in thinking, *Something is wrong with me!*—your "tree" will bear depression, negativism, a lack of confidence, anger, hostility, a controlling spirit, judgmentalism, a chip on the shoulder, hatred, and self-pity. It leads you to say to yourself, "Well, the real me is not acceptable, so I need to produce a *pretend me!*"

All the areas of your life that are out of order can be reconciled through Jesus and the work that He has done on the cross. It happened to me, and God can do it for you. Begin to believe it! Don't settle for bondage, but be determined to be free!

Here is the good news—you can be delivered from the power of rejection!

11

GOD'S WORD FOR YOU

*. . . God's love has been poured out in our hearts
through the Holy Spirit Who has been given to us.*

ROMANS 5:5

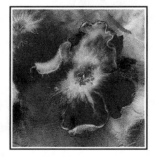

GODLY SELF-LOVE

The Bible teaches us that the love of God has been poured out in our hearts by the Holy Spirit Who has been given to us. That simply means that when the Lord, in the person of the Holy Spirit, comes to dwell in our heart because of our faith in His Son Jesus Christ, He brings love with Him, because God is love (1 John 4:8).

We all need to ask ourselves what we are doing with the love of God that has been freely given to us. Are we rejecting it because we don't think we are valuable enough to be loved? Do we believe God is like other people who have rejected and hurt us? Or are we receiving His love by faith, believing that He is greater than our failures and weaknesses?

We should love ourselves—not in a selfish, self-centered way that produces a lifestyle of self-indulgence, but in a balanced, godly way, a way that simply affirms God's creation as essentially good and right.

God's plan is this: He wants us to receive His love, love ourselves in a godly way, generously love Him in return, and finally love all the people who come into our lives.

When God reaches out to love us,
He is attempting to start a cycle that will
bless not only us but also many others.

GOD'S WORD FOR YOU

And Mephibosheth son of Jonathan, the son of Saul, came to David and fell on his face and did obeisance. David said, Mephibosheth! And he answered, Behold your servant!

David said to him, Fear not, for I will surely show you kindness for Jonathan your father's sake, and will restore to you all the land of Saul your father [grandfather], and you shall eat at my table always.

And [the cripple] bowed himself and said, What is your servant, that you should look upon such a dead dog as I am?

2 SAMUEL 9:6-8

THE DEAD-DOG IMAGE

Mephibosheth was the grandson of King Saul and the son of Jonathan, who had been a close covenant friend to David. Crippled as a youth, Mephibosheth had a poor self-image, a dead-dog image. Instead of seeing himself as the rightful heir to his father's and grandfather's legacy, he saw himself as someone who would be rejected.

When David sent for Mephibosheth, he fell down before the king and displayed fear. David told him not to fear, that he intended to show him kindness. Mephibosheth's response is an important example of the kind of poor self-image we all need to overcome.

A poor self-image causes us to operate in fear instead of faith. We look at what is wrong with us instead of what is right with Jesus. He has taken our wrongness and given us His righteousness (2 Corinthians 5:21). We need to walk in the reality of that truth.

I love the end of the story. David blessed Mephibosheth for Jonathan's sake. He gave him servants and land and provided for all of his needs.

I relate Mephibosheth's lameness to our own weaknesses. We may also fellowship and eat with our King Jesus—despite our faults and weaknesses.

We have a covenant with God, sealed and ratified in the blood of Jesus Christ.

GOD'S WORD FOR YOU

*There we saw the Nephilim [or giants], the sons of
Anak, who come from the giants; and we were in our
own sight as grasshoppers, and so we were in their sight.*

NUMBERS 13:33

ARE YOU A GRASSHOPPER?

We read in Numbers 13 of how Moses sent twelve men to scout out the Promised Land to see if it was good or bad. Ten of the men came back with what the Bible refers to as "an evil report" (Numbers 13:32). When the twelve scouts returned, they told Moses, "The land is good, but there are giants in it!"

The fear of the giants prevented God's people from entering the land that He had promised to give them. It wasn't really the giants that defeated these people; it was their poor self-image. They only saw the giants; they failed to see God.

Joshua and Caleb were the only ones who had a proper attitude toward the land. They said to Moses and the people, "Let us go up at once and possess it; we are well able to conquer it" (Numbers 13:30). In the end, they were the only ones who were allowed by God to go into the Promised Land.

God had a glorious future planned for all of the Israelites, but all of them did not enter into that future—only the ones who had a proper attitude toward God and toward themselves.

God does not have a bad attitude toward you
—you should not have one toward yourself!

GOD'S WORD FOR YOU

For I know the thoughts and plans that I have for you, says the Lord, thoughts and plans for welfare and peace and not for evil, to give you hope in your final outcome.

JEREMIAH 29:11

God Has a Plan

If you have a poor self-image, it has already adversely affected your past, but you can be healed and not allow the past to repeat itself. Let go of what lies behind, including any negative ways you have felt about yourself, and press on toward the good things God has in store for you.

God has a good plan and a purpose for each of us and a specific way and perfect time to bring it to pass, but not all of us experience it. Many times we live far below the standard that God intends for us to enjoy.

For years I did not exercise my rights and privileges as a child of God. Although I was a Christian and believed I would go to heaven when I died, I did not know that anything could be done about my past, present, or future. I had a poor self-image, and it affected my day-to-day living, as well as my outlook for the future.

Accept God's love for you and make that love the basis for your love and acceptance of yourself. Receive His affirmation, knowing that you are changing and becoming all that He desires you to be. Then start enjoying yourself—where you are—on your way to full spiritual maturity.

Let God be God in your life. Give Him the reins.
He knows what He is doing.

GOD'S WORD FOR YOU

For we are God's [own] handiwork (His workmanship), recreated in Christ Jesus, [born anew] that we may do those good works which God predestined (planned beforehand) for us [taking paths which He prepared ahead of time], that we should walk in them [living the good life which He prearranged and made ready for us to live].

EPHESIANS 2:10

*I*t's Your Choice!

Rejecting ourselves does not change us. It actually multiplies our problems. Acceptance causes us to face reality and then begin to deal with it. We cannot deal with anything as long as we are refusing to accept it or denying its reality.

God has given us a wonderful gift: *free will*. God is offering us the opportunity to accept ourselves as we are, but we have a free will and can refuse to do so if we so choose. To accept something means to view it as usual, proper, or right.

People who reject themselves do so because they cannot see themselves as proper or right. They only see their flaws and weaknesses, not their beauty and strength. This is an unbalanced attitude probably instilled by authority figures in the past who majored on what was weak and wrong rather than what was strong and right.

In Amos 3:3, we read, "Do two walk together except they make an appointment and have agreed?" To walk with God, we must agree with God. He says He loves us and accepts us; therefore, if we agree with Him, we can no longer hate and reject ourselves.

We need to agree with God that when He created us, He created something good.

GOD'S WORD FOR YOU

For the Lord corrects and disciplines everyone whom He loves, and He punishes, even scourges, every son whom He accepts and welcomes to His heart and cherishes.

You must submit to and endure [correction] for discipline; God is dealing with you as with sons. For what son is there whom his father does not [thus] train and correct and discipline?

HEBREWS 12:6-7

SELF-ACCEPTANCE ALLOWS CHANGE

Perhaps you have been struggling with accepting yourself. You see the areas in yourself that need to be changed. You desire to be like Jesus. Yet it is very difficult for you to think or say, "I accept myself." You feel that to do so would be to accept all that is wrong with you, but that is not the case.

We cannot even begin the process of change until this issue of self-acceptance is settled in our individual lives. When we truly believe that God loves us unconditionally just as we are, then we will be willing to receive His correction.

Change requires correction—people who do not know they are loved have a very difficult time receiving correction. In order for God to change us, He must correct us. We may hear His correction and even agree with it, but it will only make us feel angry or condemned unless we know it is ultimately going to bring about the change that is needed in our life.

To grow up in God and be changed, we must trust Him. Often He will lead us in ways that we cannot understand, and during those times we must have a tight grip on His love for us.

Be patient with yourself. Keep pressing on and believe that you are changing every day.

GOD'S WORD FOR YOU

*Do not be conformed to this world (this age),
[fashioned after and adapted to its external, superficial
customs], but be transformed (changed) by the [entire]
renewal of your mind [by its new ideals and its new
attitude], so that you may prove [for yourselves] what is
the good and acceptable and perfect will of God, even the
thing which is good and acceptable and perfect [in His
sight for you].*

ROMANS 12:2

"How Can I Change?"

Change does not come through struggle, human effort without God, frustration, self-hatred, self-rejection, guilt, or works of the flesh.

Change in our lives comes as a result of having our minds renewed by the Word of God. As we agree with God and really believe that what He says is true, it gradually begins to manifest itself in us. We begin to think differently, then we begin to talk differently, and finally we begin to act differently. This is a process that develops in stages, and we must always remember that while it is taking place we can still have the attitude, "I'm OK, and I'm on my way!"

Enjoy yourself while you are changing. Enjoy where you are on the way to where you are going. Enjoy the journey! Don't waste all of your "now time" trying to rush into the future. Remember, tomorrow will have troubles of its own (Matthew 6:34).

Relax. Let God be God. Stop being so hard on yourself. Change is a process; it comes little by little.

*We can come to Jesus just as we are.
He takes us "as is" and makes
us what we ought to be.*

HEALING
FOR DAMAGED
EMOTIONS

*Jesus longs to heal our broken hearts
and lavish His great love upon us.*

GOD'S WORD FOR YOU

The Spirit of the Lord God is upon me, because the Lord has anointed and qualified me to preach the Gospel of good tidings to the meek, the poor, and afflicted; He has sent me to bind up and heal the brokenhearted, to proclaim liberty to the [physical and spiritual] captives and the opening of the prison and of the eyes to those who are bound, [Rom. 10:15.]

To proclaim the acceptable year of the Lord [the year of His favor] and the day of vengeance of our God, to comfort all who mourn, [Matt. 11:2-6; Luke 4:18, 19; 7:22.]

To grant [consolation and joy] to those who mourn in Zion—to give them an ornament (a garland or diadem) of beauty instead of ashes, the oil of joy instead of mourning, the garment [expressive] of praise instead of a heavy, burdened, and failing spirit—that they may be called oaks of righteousness [lofty, strong, and magnificent, distinguished for uprightness, justice, and right standing with God], the planting of the Lord, that He may be glorified.

ISAIAH 61:1-3

t w o

HEALING FOR DAMAGED EMOTIONS

motional healing, also referred to as inner healing, is a subject that needs to be talked about in a scriptural, balanced way that produces godly results. Our inner life is much more important than our outer life. The apostle Paul said in 2 Corinthians 4:16 that even though our outer man is progressively decaying and wasting away, our inner self is being progressively renewed day after day. Romans 14:17 lets us know that the Kingdom of God is not meat and drink (not outward things), but it is righteousness, peace, and joy in the Holy Spirit, and Luke 17:21 says the Kingdom of God is within you.

I was sexually, physically, verbally, and emotionally abused from the time I can remember until I finally left home at the age of eighteen. I have been rejected, abandoned, and betrayed. I, too, was an "emotional prisoner" for a long time, but God has healed and transformed me with His love. And He will do the same for you!

In Isaiah 61 the Lord said that He came to heal the brokenhearted. I believe that means those broken inside, those crushed and wounded inwardly. Jesus wants to lead us out of emotional devastation to health and wholeness in the inner man by the power of the Holy Spirit.

Wherever you are spiritually or emotionally, God will meet you where you are.

GOD'S WORD FOR YOU

And I am convinced and sure of this very thing, that He Who began a good work in you will continue until the day of Jesus Christ [right up to the time of His return], developing [that good work] and perfecting and bringing it to full completion in you.

PHILIPPIANS 1:6-7

ONE STEP AT A TIME

When I speak on the healing of emotional wounds, I like to hold up several different-colored shoestrings tied together in a knot. I tell the audience, "This is you when you first start the process of transformation with God. You're all knotted up. Each knot represents a different problem in your life. Untangling those knots and straightening out those problems is going to take a bit of time and effort, so don't get discouraged if it doesn't happen all at once."

If you want to receive emotional healing and come into an area of wholeness, you must realize that healing is a process. Allow the Lord to deal with you and your problems in His way and in His time. Your part is to cooperate with Him in whatever area He chooses to start dealing with you first.

In our modern, instantaneous society we expect everything to be quick and easy. The Lord never gets in a hurry, and He never quits. Sometimes it may seem that you are not making any progress. That's because the Lord is untying your knots one at a time. The process may be hard and take time, but if you will "stick with the program," sooner or later you will see the victory and experience the freedom you have wanted so long.

God wants you to believe and keep pressing on.

GOD'S WORD FOR YOU

For we do not have a High Priest Who is unable to understand and sympathize and have a shared feeling with our weaknesses and infirmities and liability to the assaults of temptation, but One Who has been tempted in every respect as we are, yet without sinning.

HEBREWS 4:15

JESUS AND EMOTIONS

According to the writer of Hebrews, Jesus experienced every emotion and suffered every feeling you and I do, yet without sinning. He did not sin because He did not give in to His wrong feelings. He knew the Word of God in every area of life because He spent years studying it before He began His ministry. You and I will never be able to say no to our feelings if we don't have a strong knowledge of God's Word.

When I am hurt by someone and I feel angry or upset, I pray, "Jesus, I am so glad that You understand what I am feeling right now and that You don't condemn me for feeling this way. I don't want to give vent to my emotions. Help me to forgive those who have wronged me and not slight them, avoid them, or seek to pay them back for the harm they have done me."

God wants us to be more sensitive to the feelings and needs of others and less sensitive to our own feelings and needs. He wants us to deposit ourselves in His hands and let Him take care of us while we are practicing being kind and compassionate and sensitive to other people.

❧

Make your emotions serve you
—don't spend your life serving them.

GOD'S WORD FOR YOU

*For no temptation (no trial regarded as enticing to sin,
no matter how it comes or where it leads) has overtaken
you and laid hold on you that is not common to man [that
is, no temptation or trial has come to you that is beyond
human resistance and that is not adjusted and adapted
and belonging to human experience, and such as man
can bear]. But God is faithful [to His Word and to His
compassionate nature], and He [can be trusted] not to let
you be tempted and tried and assayed beyond your ability
and strength of resistance and power to endure, but with
the temptation He will [always] also provide the way out
(the means of escape to a landing place), that you may
be capable and strong and powerful to bear up under it
patiently.*

1 CORINTHIANS 10:13

No Pain, No Gain!

In moving from devastation to emotional wholeness, even with the Holy Spirit leading us, the pain of the healing process from emotional wounds can be more traumatic than experiencing physical pain. Because I experienced so much emotional pain, I grew weary of hurting. I was attempting to find healing by following the leadership of the Holy Spirit. Yet I could not understand why the process had to be so painful. The Lord showed me how that each time I went through one of the painful events or situations (being sexually abused at home, being ridiculed at school, being subjected to constant fear), it was like a new doorway of pain.

The Lord revealed to me that I had been hiding behind many such "doorways of pain." I was *deep* in bondage, taking refuge behind false personalities, pretenses, and facades. I began to understand that when people are led out of bondage into freedom, they must pass back through similar doorways of pain to get on the other side of those doors. They pass through, not actual experiences such as abuse, but the emotional responses to the experiences. To deliver and heal, the Lord must lead us to face issues, people, and truths that we find difficult, if not impossible, to face on our own.

Remember, God will never allow a temptation to come upon you that you are not able to bear.

GOD'S WORD FOR YOU

*There was a certain man there who had suffered with
a deep-seated and lingering disorder for thirty-eight years.*
When Jesus noticed him lying there [helpless],
knowing that he had already been a long time in that
condition, He said to him, Do you want to become well?
[Are you really in earnest about getting well?]

JOHN 5:5-6

DO YOU WANT TO GET WELL?

Isn't this an amazing question for Jesus to ask this poor man who had been sick for thirty-eight long years: "Do you really want to become well?" That is the Lord's question to each of us as well.

Do you know there are people who really don't want to get well? They only want to talk about their problem. Are you one of those people? Do you really want to get well, or do you just want to talk about your problem? Sometimes people get addicted to having a problem. It becomes their identity, their life. It defines everything they think and say and do. All their being is centered around that particular problem.

If you have a "deep-seated and lingering disorder," the Lord wants you to know that it does not have to be the central focal point of your entire existence. He wants you to trust Him and cooperate with Him as He leads you to victory over that problem one step at a time.

Whatever our problem may be, God has promised to meet our need and to repay us for our loss. Facing truth is the key to unlocking prison doors that may have held us in bondage.

God yearns to see you become all that He has planned for you to be.

GOD'S WORD FOR YOU

*If you abide in My word [hold fast to My teachings
and live in accordance with them], you are truly My
disciples.*

*And you will know the Truth, and the Truth will set
you free.*

JOHN 8:31-32

Face the Truth

If you are to receive emotional healing and restoration of your broken spirit, you must learn to face the truth. You cannot be set free while living in denial. You cannot pretend either that certain negative events did not happen to you, or that you have not been influenced by them or reacted in response to them.

Many times people who have suffered abuse or some other tragedy in their lives try to act as though it never happened. Early traumatic experiences can cause us to be emotionally damaged and wounded in later life because we develop opinions and attitudes about ourselves based on what we did.

From my own experience, as well as my years of ministry to others, I have come to realize that we human beings are marvelously adept at building walls and cramming things into dark corners, pretending they never happened.

It is so wonderful to have Jesus as a friend, because we don't have to hide anything from Him. He already knows everything about us anyway. We can always come to Him and know we will be loved and accepted no matter what we have suffered or how we have reacted to it.

Even though it may be hard to face the truth, Jesus promises to be with us and set us free.

GOD'S WORD FOR YOU

But be doers of the Word [obey the message], and not merely listeners to it, betraying yourselves [into deception by reasoning contrary to the Truth].

JAMES 1:22

Listen to and obey My voice, and I will be your God and you will be My people; and walk in the whole way that I command you, that it may be well with you.

JEREMIAH 7:23

OBEY THE WORD

I recall a woman who attended one of my seminars. She desperately wanted to be free of the emotional wounds that had left her insecure and fearful, but nothing seemed to work for her. At the conclusion of the seminar, she told me that she now understood why she had never experienced any progress.

She said, "Joyce, I sat with a group of ladies who had a lot of the same problems that I did. Step by step God had been delivering them. As I listened, I heard them say, 'God led me to do this, and I did it. Then He led me to another thing, and I did it.' I realized that God had also told me to do the same things. The only difference was they did what He said to do, and I didn't."

To receive what God promises us in His Word, we must obey the Word. We must become doers of the Word and not hearers only. Obeying the Word requires consistency and diligence. It can't be hit or miss. We can't just do it for a while to see if it works. There must be a dedication and commitment to do the Word whatever the outcome.

God's way works!
And there is no other way that does.

GOD'S WORD FOR YOU

*Confess to one another therefore your faults (your
slips, your false steps, your offenses, your sins) and pray
[also] for one another, that you may be healed and
restored [to a spiritual tone of mind and heart].*

JAMES 5:16

Confess Your Faults

I think there is a place for eventually sharing with someone else that which has occurred in our life. There is something tremendously healing about verbalizing it to another person that does wonders for us.

But use wisdom. Be Spirit-led. Choose someone you know you can trust. Be sure that by sharing your burden with someone else, you do not place it upon that individual's shoulders. Also don't go on a digging expedition, trying to dig up old injuries long buried and forgotten.

It is so important to use wisdom and balance in these matters. If you are going to share your problems with someone, let God show you whom to choose as a confidant. Pick a mature believer, someone who is not going to be burdened down or harmed by what you share or use it to hurt you or make you feel worse about yourself.

Many times there is a release that comes to us when we finally tell someone else those secrets that have been crammed in the background of our lives for years, especially when we discover that the person with whom we share them still loves and accepts us in spite of them.

*Bringing things out in the open
causes them to lose their grip on us.*

GOD'S WORD FOR YOU

For I will forgive their iniquity, and I will [seriously] remember their sin no more.

JEREMIAH 31:34

As far as the east is from the west, so far has He removed our transgressions from us.

PSALM 103:12

RECEIVE FORGIVENESS AND FORGET YOUR SIN

No matter what your problem or how bad you feel about yourself as a result of it, God loves you. In Jesus Christ He has given you a new life. He has given you a new family and new friends to love and accept and appreciate and support you. You are okay, and you are going to make it because of the One Who lives on the inside of you and cares for you.

You may have had an abortion, but you need to look in the mirror and confess, "I did that, Lord, and it is a marvel to me to realize that I can stand here and look myself in the eye. But I can do so because I know that even though I did that horrible sin, You have put my sins as far away from me as the east is from the west, and You remember them no more!"

Once we have confessed our sins and asked for God's forgiveness, if we continue to drag them up to Him every time we go to Him in prayer, we are reminding Him of something He has not only *forgiven* but also actually *forgotten*.

❧

God's mercy is new every morning.
Each day we can find a fresh place to begin.

45

CONFIDENCE

*Confidence in Christ is required for us
to truly succeed at being ourselves.*

GOD'S WORD FOR YOU

[Most] blessed is the man who believes in, trusts in, and relies on the Lord, and whose hope and confidence the Lord is.

JEREMIAH 17:7

three

CONFIDENCE

o succeed at being ourselves, we must be confident. It is not self-confidence we are to seek, but confidence in Christ. I like *The Amplified Bible* translation of Philippians 4:13, which says, ". . . I am self-sufficient in Christ's sufficiency." It is actually a sin to be confident in ourselves—but to be confident in Christ should be the goal of every believer.

Jesus said, ". . . apart from Me [cut off from vital union with Me] you can do nothing" (John 15:5). We keep attempting to do things in the strength of our own flesh, instead of placing all our confidence in Him.

Most of our internal agony, our struggling and frustration, comes from misplaced confidence. In Philippians 3:3, Paul says that we are to put no confidence in the flesh. This means our own selves as well as our friends and family. I am not saying that we cannot trust anyone, but if we give to others the trust that belongs to God alone, we will not experience victory. God will not allow us to succeed until our confidence is in the right place, or more correctly, in the right Person.

Jesus is the Rock—the only true source of stability. Put your trust in Him.

GOD'S WORD FOR YOU

[God] disarmed the principalities and powers that were ranged against us and made a bold display and public example of them, in triumphing over them in Him and in it [the cross].

COLOSSIANS 2:15

GET RID OF THE FAILURE SYNDROME

People who have been abused, rejected, or abandoned usually lack confidence. Such individuals are shame-based and guilt-ridden and have a very poor self-image. The devil knows that and begins his assault on personal confidence whenever and wherever he can find an opening. His ultimate goal is total destruction of the person.

The devil knows that an individual without confidence will never step out to do anything edifying for the Kingdom of God or detrimental to Satan's kingdom. He does not want you to fulfill God's plan for your life. If he can make you believe that you are incapable, then you won't even try to accomplish anything worthwhile. Even if you do make an effort, your fear of failure will seal your defeat, which, because of your lack of confidence, you probably expected from the beginning. This is often what is referred to as the "Failure Syndrome."

God wants you to know that the devil is already a defeated foe. Jesus triumphed over him on the cross and made a public display of his disgrace in the spirit realm. Jesus' victory means you can get rid of the failure syndrome. His ability to bring His will to pass in your life is determined by your faith in Him and in His Word.

God's victory purchased on the cross is total and complete.

51

GOD'S WORD FOR YOU

Lean on, trust in, and be confident in the Lord with all your heart and mind and do not rely on your own insight or understanding.

In all your ways know, recognize, and acknowledge Him, and He will direct and make straight and plain your paths.

PROVERBS 3:5-6

THE LIE ABOUT SELF-CONFIDENCE

Everyone talks about self-confidence. All kinds of seminars are available on confidence, both in the secular world and the church world. Confidence is generally referred to as "self-confidence" because we all know that we need to feel good about ourselves if we are ever to accomplish anything in life. We have been taught that all people have a basic need to believe in themselves. However, that is not the truth.

Actually, we don't need to believe in ourselves— we need to believe in Jesus in us. We don't dare feel good about ourselves apart from Him.

If we believe the lie of self-confidence, we will create many complicated problems. We will never reach our full potential in Christ; we will live ruled by fear without knowing true joy, fulfillment, or satisfaction, and will lose sight of our right to be an individual. The Holy Spirit will be grieved.

Don't be concerned about yourself, your weaknesses, or your strengths. Get your eyes off of yourself and onto the Lord. If you are weak, He can strengthen you. If you have any strength, it is because He gave it to you. So either way, your eyes should be on Him and not on yourself.

❧

We do not need self-confidence;
we need God-confidence!

GOD'S WORD FOR YOU

Thus says the Lord: Cursed [with great evil] is the strong man who trusts in and relies on frail man, making weak [human] flesh his arm, and whose mind and heart turn aside from the Lord.

JEREMIAH 17:5

HAVE CONFIDENCE IN GOD ALONE

In order to succeed at anything, we must have confidence, but first and foremost it must be confidence in God, not confidence in anything else. We must develop confidence in God's love, goodness, and mercy. We must believe that He wants us to succeed.

God did not create us for failure. We may fail at some things on our way to success, but if we trust Him, He will take even our mistakes and work them out for our good (Romans 8:28).

Hebrews 3:6 tells us we must ". . . hold fast and firm to the end our joyful and exultant confidence and sense of triumph in our hope [in Christ]." It is important to realize that a mistake is not the end of things if we hold on to our confidence.

We all have a destiny, but just because we are destined to do something does not mean that it will automatically happen. I went through many things while God was developing me and my ministry. Often I lost my confidence concerning the call on my life. Each time I had to get my confidence back before I could go forward again.

Put your confidence in God alone, and He will cause you to truly succeed at being yourself.

GOD'S WORD FOR YOU

The man who through faith is just and upright . . .
shall live by faith.

ROMANS 1:17

 BE CONSISTENTLY CONFIDENT

Confidence is actually faith in God. We must learn to be consistently confident, not occasionally confident.

I had to learn to remain confident when I was told by friends and family that a woman should not be preaching the Word of God. I knew God had called me to preach His Word, but I was still affected by the rejection of people. I had to grow in confidence to the place where people's opinions and their acceptance or rejection did not affect my confidence level. My confidence had to be in God, not in people.

Romans 1:17 tells us that we can go from faith to faith. I spent many years going from faith to doubt to unbelief and then back to faith. Then I realized that when I lose my confidence, I leave a door open for the devil. If I allow him to steal my confidence, I suddenly have no faith to minister to people.

If you want to succeed, you must be consistently confident. Be confident about your gifts and calling, your ability in Christ. Believe you hear from God and that you are led by the Holy Spirit. Be bold in the Lord. See yourself as a winner in Him!

Don't look to your insecurities; look to God and be confident. He is your strength and salvation.

GOD'S WORD FOR YOU

Yet amid all these things we are more than conquerors and gain a surpassing victory through Him Who loved us.

ROMANS 8:37

More Than Conquerors

We need to have a sense of triumph. Paul assures us that through Christ Jesus we are more than conquerors. Believing that truth gives us confidence.

Sometimes our confidence is shaken when trials come, especially if they are lengthy. We should have so much confidence in God's love for us that no matter what comes against us, we know deep inside that we are more than conquerors. If we are truly confident, we have no need to fear trouble, challenges, or trying times, because we know they will pass.

Whenever a trial of any kind comes against you, always remember: *This too shall pass!* Be confident that during the trial you will learn something that will help you in the future.

Without confidence we are stifled at every turn. Satan drops a bomb, and our dreams are destroyed. Eventually we start over, but we never make much progress. But those who know they are more than conquerors through Jesus Christ make rapid progress.

We must take a step of faith and decide to be confident in all things in Him. Confident people get the job done. They are fulfilled because they are succeeding at being themselves.

We will not succeed at being ourselves until our confidence is in God.

GOD'S WORD FOR YOU

*David was greatly distressed, for the men spoke of
stoning him because the souls of them all were bitterly
grieved, each man for his sons and daughters. But David
encouraged and strengthened himself in the Lord his God.*

1 SAMUEL 30:6

THE TORMENT OF SELF-DOUBT

If we don't believe in ourselves, who is going to? God believes in us, and it's a good thing too; otherwise, we might never make any progress. We cannot wait for someone else to come along and encourage us to be all we can be.

When David and his men found themselves in a seemingly hopeless situation, which the men blamed on him, David encouraged and strengthened himself in the Lord. Later on, that situation was totally turned around (1 Samuel 30:1-20).

When David was just a boy, everyone around him discouraged him concerning his ability to fight Goliath. They told him he was too young and too inexperienced, and he didn't have the right armor or the right weapons. But David knew his God and had confidence in Him. David believed that God would be strong in his weakness and give him the victory.

Self-doubt is absolutely tormenting, and we must rid ourselves of it. Like David, we must learn to know our God—about His love, His ways, and His Word—then ultimately we must *decide* whether we believe or not. When we don't doubt ourselves but trust in God, He will give us the victory.

The way to end the torment of self-doubt is to look to God and have faith in His mighty power.

GOD'S WORD FOR YOU

Having gifts (faculties, talents, qualities) that differ according to the grace given us, let us use them: [He whose gift is] prophecy, [let him prophesy] according to the proportion of his faith;

[He whose gift is] practical service, let him give himself to serving; he who teaches, to his teaching;

He who exhorts (encourages), to his exhortation; he who contributes, let him do it in simplicity and liberality; he who gives aid and superintends, with zeal and singleness of mind; he who does acts of mercy, with genuine cheerfulness and joyful eagerness.

ROMANS 12:6-8

❧

The sun is glorious in one way, the moon is glorious in another way, and the stars are glorious in their own [distinctive] way; for one star differs from and surpasses another in its beauty and brilliance.

1 CORINTHIANS 15:41

❧

CONFIDENT TO BE DIFFERENT

We are all different. Like the sun, the moon, and the stars, God has created us to be different from one another, and He has done it on purpose. Each of us meets a need, and we are all part of God's overall plan. When we struggle to be like others, we lose ourselves, and we grieve the Holy Spirit. God wants us to fit into His plan, not to feel pressured trying to fit into everyone else's plans. It is all right to be different.

We are all born with different temperaments, different physical features, different fingerprints, different gifts and abilities. Our goal should be to find out what we individually are supposed to be, and then succeed at being that.

Romans 12 teaches us to give ourselves to our gift. We are to find out what we are good at and then throw ourselves wholeheartedly into it.

We should be free to love and accept ourselves and one another without feeling pressure to compare or compete. Secure people who know God loves them and has a plan for them are not threatened by the abilities of others. They enjoy what other people can do, and they enjoy what they can do.

✦

God gave you gifts and wants you to focus on your potential instead of your limitations.

GOD'S WORD FOR YOU

Whoever finds his [lower] life will lose it [the higher life], and whoever loses his [lower] life on My account will find it [the higher life].

MATTHEW 10:39

Don't Lose Yourself

How can we succeed at being ourselves if we don't know ourselves? Life is like a maze sometimes, and it is easy to get lost. Everyone, it seems, expects something different from us. There is pressure coming at us from every direction to keep others happy and meet their needs.

We then attempt to become what they want us to be. In the process, we may lose ourselves. We may fail to discover what God's intention is for us. We try so hard to please everyone else and yet not be pleased ourselves.

For years I tried to be so many things that I wasn't that I got myself totally confused. I had to get off the merry-go-round and ask myself: "Who am I living for? Why am I doing all these things? Have I become a people-pleaser? Am I really in God's will for my life?"

Have you also lost yourself? Are you frustrated from trying to meet all the demands of other people while feeling unfulfilled yourself? You need to take a stand and be determined to know your identity, your direction, and your calling—God's will for your life. You will find yourself by finding His will for your life and doing it.

If you give your heart to doing His will, you'll find your true self.

DEVELOP
YOUR
POTENTIAL

*We are free to develop our potential
because of what God has done
through Christ for us!*

GOD'S WORD FOR YOU

Do you not know that in a race all the runners compete, but [only] one receives the prize? So run [your race] that you may lay hold [of the prize] and make it yours.

1 CORINTHIANS 9:24

four

DEVELOP YOUR POTENTIAL

hen we are confident and free from tormenting fears and self-doubt, we are able to develop our potential and succeed at being all God intended us to be. But we cannot develop our potential if we fear failure. We will be so afraid of failing or making mistakes that it will prevent us from stepping out.

I often see people who have great potential, and yet when opportunities and promotions are offered them, they quickly turn them down. In many cases, they are insecure and unaware of how much they could accomplish for the Kingdom of God if they would only step out in faith and confidence.

When we are insecure, frequently we will stay with what is safe and familiar rather than taking a chance on stepping out and failing. We avoid accepting greater responsibility, and the truth is that none of us is ever ready. But when God is ready to move in our lives, we need to believe that He will equip us with what we need at the time we need it.

Humbly leaning on God leads to success. If our confidence is in Christ rather than ourselves, we are free to develop our potential, because we are free from the fear of failure.

The development and manifestation of potential requires firm faith, not wishful thinking.

GOD'S WORD FOR YOU

Any enterprise is built by wise planning, becomes strong through common sense, and profits wonderfully by keeping abreast of the facts.

PROVERBS 24:3-4 TLB

Don't Make Small Plans!

I hope you have a dream or a vision in your heart for something greater than what you have now. It is important to have dreams and visions for our lives. We atrophy without something to reach for. God has created us to have goals. Ephesians 3:20 KJV tells us that God is "able to do exceedingly abundantly above all we can ask or think." We need to think big thoughts, hope for big things, and ask for big things.

Quite often we look at a task and think there is no way we can do what needs to be done. That happens because we look at ourselves when we should be looking at God.

When the Lord called Joshua to take the place of Moses and lead the Israelites into the Promised Land, He said to him, "As I was with Moses, so I will be with you; I will not fail you or forsake you" (Joshua 1:5).

If God promises to be with us—and He does—that is really all we need. His strength is made perfect in our weakness (2 Corinthians 12:9 KJV). Whatever ingredients we are lacking in the natural man, He adds to the spiritual man.

God is honored when we believe Him to do the "big things" we have dreamed about.

GOD'S WORD FOR YOU

. . . be strong in the Lord [be empowered through your union with Him]; draw your strength from Him [that strength which His boundless might provides].

EPHESIANS 6:10

. . . they that wait upon the Lord shall renew their strength; they shall mount up with wings as eagles; they shall run, and not be weary; and they shall walk, and not faint.

ISAIAH 40:31 KJV

DRAW UPON THE STRENGTH OF THE LORD

When God called me into ministry, I wanted to fulfill His call more than anything. I didn't even know where to begin, let alone how to finish the task. As God gave me anointed ideas and opened to me doors of opportunity for service, I stepped out in faith. Each time He met me with the strength, wisdom, and ability that was needed to be successful.

If you're going to learn to be successful in the task that God sets before you, you have to learn the secret of drawing on His strength. Your strength will run out, but His never will.

In Ephesians 6:10, Paul assures us that the Holy Spirit will pour strength into our human spirit as we fellowship with Him. And the prophet Isaiah says that those who have learned the secret of waiting on the Lord "shall mount up with wings as eagles" (Isaiah 40:31). It is very obvious from these scriptures that we are strengthened as we go to God for what we are lacking.

Everything we are and need is found "in Christ." In Him we are redeemed. In Him we are complete. Our wisdom, strength, peace, and hope are in Him. Our everything is in Him!

God does not just want to give you strength —He wants to be your strength.

GOD'S WORD FOR YOU

. . . let us strip off and throw aside every encumbrance (unnecessary weight) and that sin which so readily (deftly and cleverly) clings to and entangles us, and let us run with patient endurance and steady and active persistence the appointed course of the race that is set before us.

HEBREWS 12:1

$\mathcal{R}$UNNING THE RACE

When the writer of the letter to the Hebrews told them to *strip off and throw aside every encumbrance*, he was thinking of the runners in his day who entered races with the intention of winning. They literally stripped off their clothes down to a simple loincloth. They made sure nothing could entangle them and prevent them from running their fastest. They were running to win!

To develop our potential and succeed at becoming all that God intended us to be, we must take an inventory of our life and prune off anything that entangles us or simply steals our time. Hebrews 12:1 tells us to strip off and throw aside every encumbrance and the *sin* that entangles us. It is virtually impossible to be a spiritual success with known, willful sin in our lives. We must have an aggressive attitude about keeping sin out of our lives.

When God says something is wrong, then it is wrong. We don't need to discuss, theorize, blame, make excuses, or feel sorry for ourselves—we need to agree with God, ask for forgiveness, and obey the Holy Spirit to get that sin out of our lives forever.

Lay aside everything that hinders
and run the race of holiness.
The reward is God Himself!

GOD'S WORD FOR YOU

Do you not know that in a race all the runners compete, but [only] one receives the prize? So run [your race] that you may lay hold [of the prize] and make it yours.

Now every athlete who goes into training conducts himself temperately and restricts himself in all things. They do it to win a wreath that will soon wither, but we [do it to receive a crown of eternal blessedness] that cannot wither.

Therefore I do not run uncertainly (without definite aim). I do not box like one beating the air and striking without an adversary.

But [like a boxer] I buffet my body [handle it roughly, discipline it by hardships] and subdue it, for fear that after proclaiming to others the Gospel and things pertaining to it, I myself should become unfit [not stand the test, be unapproved and rejected as a counterfeit].

1 CORINTHIANS 9:24-27

$\mathscr{B}$E TEMPERATE IN ALL THINGS

Those of us who intend to run the race to win must conduct ourselves temperately and restrict ourselves in all things. We cannot expect someone else to make us do what is right. We must listen to the Holy Spirit and take action ourselves.

Paul said he buffeted his body. Paul was running the race to win! He knew he could not develop his potential without bringing his body, mind, and emotions under control.

Self-discipline is the most important feature in any life, especially in the life of the Christian. Unless we discipline our minds, our mouths, and our emotions, we will live in ruin. One major emotion many need to learn to rule is their temper.

We can never achieve our full potential if our flesh is controlling our emotions. If we are truly intent on running the race, we must resist negative emotions. There are many negative emotions other than just anger, and we must be ready to take authority over them as soon as they rear their ugly heads.

We must allow the Holy Spirit to replace all those destructive emotions with His fruit: "love, joy, peace, patience, kindness, goodness, faithfulness, gentleness, self-control" (Galatians 5:22-23 NASB).

Self-improvement does not come through self-effort; it comes from dependence upon the Holy Spirit.

GOD'S WORD FOR YOU

For who has known the mind of the Lord and who has understood His thoughts, or who has [ever] been His counselor? [Isa. 40:13, 14.]

ROMANS 11:34

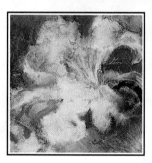

God's Way Is Better

We need to come to the realization that God is smarter than we are. No matter what you or I may think, God's way is better than ours. We often think we know what's best, and then we throw all our flesh into bringing it to pass.

Often we experience a lot of disappointment, which hinders joy and enjoyment, due to deciding for ourselves that something has to be done a certain way or by a certain time. When we want something very strongly, we can easily convince ourselves that it is God's will.

God has no need of a counselor to tell Him what He should do for us. His will is perfect, and He has good plans for us to become all that He intends us to be. The prophet Jeremiah says, "For I know the thoughts and plans that I have for you, says the Lord, thoughts and plans for welfare and peace and not for evil, to give you hope in your final outcome" (Jeremiah 29:11).

When we face puzzling situations, we should say, "Well, Lord, this does not make any sense to me right now, but I trust You. I believe You love me and that You are doing what is best for me."

God does not need our counsel in order to work;
He needs our faith.

GOD'S WORD FOR YOU

My brethren, count it all joy when you fall into various trials, knowing that the testing of your faith produces patience. But let patience have its perfect work, that you may be perfect and complete, lacking nothing.

JAMES 1:2-4 NKJV

And let us not be weary in well doing: for in due season we shall reap, if we faint not.

GALATIANS 6:9 KJV

WAIT ON GOD'S PERFECT TIMING

As God is working out His perfect plan for us, we often want it to happen right now. But character development takes time and patience.

James tells us that when patience has had its perfect work, we will be perfect (fully developed) and complete, lacking nothing. It also speaks about trials of all kinds, and it is during these trials that we are instructed to be patient. Patience is not the ability to wait. It is the ability to keep a good attitude while waiting. Patience is a fruit of the Spirit that manifests itself in a calm, positive attitude despite the circumstances.

"Due season" is God's season, not ours. We are in a hurry, but God isn't. He takes time to do things right—He lays a solid foundation before He attempts to build a building. We are God's building under construction. He is the Master Builder, and He knows what He is doing. God's timing seems to be His own little secret. The Bible promises us that He will never be late, but I have also discovered that He is usually not early. It seems that He takes every available opportunity to develop the fruit of patience in us.

Our potential is only developed
as our patience is developed.

GOD'S WORD FOR YOU

*Are you so foolish and so senseless and so silly?
Having begun [your new life spiritually] with the [Holy]
Spirit, are you now reaching perfection [by dependence]
on the flesh?*

*Have you suffered so many things and experienced so
much all for nothing (to no purpose)—if it really is to no
purpose and in vain?*

*Then does He Who supplies you with His marvelous
[Holy] Spirit and works powerfully and miraculously
among you do so on [the grounds of your doing] what the
Law demands, or because of your believing in and
adhering to and trusting in and relying on the message that
you heard?*

GALATIANS 3:3-5

BEGUN BY FAITH, FINISHED BY FAITH

We need to ask ourselves what Paul was asking the "foolish," "senseless," and "silly" Galatians: Having begun our new lives in Christ by dependence on the Spirit, are we now trying to live them in the flesh?

Just as we are saved by grace (God's unmerited favor) through faith, and not by works of the flesh (Ephesians 2:8-9), so we need to learn to live by grace through faith, and not by works of the flesh.

When we were saved, we were in no condition to help ourselves. What kind of condition are we in now that we have been saved by grace through faith in the finished work of Jesus Christ? We still are in no condition to help ourselves. We have to completely run out of trying to make this new life work by our own effort. Until we are thoroughly convinced we can't do it, we will be doing what the foolish Galatians were trying to do: *live the new life by effort in the flesh*.

The flesh profits us nothing. Only the Spirit can cause us to grow up into the perfection of Christ.

*It is the power of the Holy Spirit
that enables us to live this new life.*

GOD'S WORD FOR YOU

*And all of us, as with unveiled face, [because we]
continued to behold [in the Word of God] as in a mirror
the glory of the Lord, are constantly being transfigured
into His very own image in ever increasing splendor and
from one degree of glory to another; [for this comes] from
the Lord [Who is] the Spirit.*

2 CORINTHIANS 3:18

From Glory to Glory

How do you see yourself?

Are you able to honestly evaluate yourself and your behavior and not come under condemnation? Are you able to look at how far you still have to go, but also at how far you have come? Where you are now is not where you will end up. Have a vision for the finish line, or you will never get out of the starting block.

In 2 Corinthians 3:18, Paul states that God changes us "from one degree of glory to another." In other words, the changes in us personally, as well as those in our circumstances, take place in degrees.

You are in a glory right now!

If you are born again, then you are somewhere on the path of the righteous. You may not be as far along as you would like to be, but thank God you are on the path. You now belong to the household of God and are being transformed by Him day by day. Enjoy the glory you are in right now and don't get jealous of where others may be. I don't believe we pass into the next degree of glory until we have learned to enjoy the one we are in at the moment.

❧

Don't be too hard on yourself. God is changing you day by day as you trust Him.

EXPERIENCING THE LOVE OF GOD

*God's love for you is the foundation
for your faith, for your freedom
from sin, and for your ability
to minister to others without fear.*

GOD'S WORD FOR YOU

In this the love of God was made manifest (displayed) where we are concerned: in that God sent His Son, the only begotten or unique [Son], into the world so that we might live through Him.

1 JOHN 4:9

EXPERIENCING THE LOVE OF GOD

ave you ever asked yourself, "Am I lovable?" You may have immediately said, "No, I'm not!"

I thought I was unlovable before I came to understand the true nature of God's love and His reason for loving me. I was impatient with people, legalistic and harsh, judgmental, rude, selfish, and unforgiving. A breakthrough came in my life when God began to show me that I could not love others because I had never received His love for me. I acknowledged the Bible teaching that God loved me, but it was not a reality in my heart.

God can love us because He wants to; it pleases Him. Just as it is impossible for God not to love, so it is impossible for us to do anything to keep Him from loving us. Once you realize that you are loved by God, not because of anything you are or anything you have done, then you can quit trying to deserve His love or earn His love and simply receive it and enjoy it.

Once your heart is filled with the knowledge of God's awesome unconditional love, you can begin to love Him in return: *We love Him, because He first loved us.*

Knowing that God loves you gives you confidence in Him and trust in His faithfulness.

GOD'S WORD FOR YOU

For [if we are] in Christ Jesus, neither circumcision nor uncircumcision counts for anything, but only faith activated and energized and expressed and working through love.

GALATIANS 5:6

*L*OVE, TRUST, AND FAITH

Stop trying so hard to get faith and please God, and start spending all that time and effort with God, loving Him. We are only going to be able to walk in faith based on what we believe about our relationship with God.

Galatians 5:6 says that faith works by love. Faith will not work without love. Everybody thinks that this scripture means that if they don't love other people, their faith won't work. What it means is that if they don't know how much God loves them, their faith won't work.

Trusting God and walking in faith is leaning on Him and trusting Him for everything. You can't do that with someone if you don't know he loves you. You have the love of God inside you, and all you need is to begin to recognize it when He shows you. The Bible says, "We love Him, because He first loved us" (1 John 4:19). It would be impossible for you to love God if you weren't assured of the fact that He loved you first.

It is all down inside you, in your heart. God loves you! You are wonderful! You are precious! Nobody in all the world will ever love you as God loves you.

Faith works by letting God love you.

GOD'S WORD FOR YOU

In this is love: not that we loved God, but that He loved us and sent His Son to be the propitiation (the atoning sacrifice) for our sins.

1 JOHN 4:10

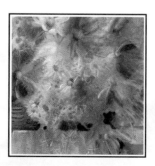

God's Love Will Change You

Meditate on God's love for you. That's what is going to change you. If you don't like something about yourself, *"knowing that you know"* that God loves you is going to change it.

God wants you to spend time with Him in fellowship and worship on a daily basis. That's what will change you. It is the private time you spend with God, just loving Him and letting Him love you, that is going to cause you to grow up and be strong in your spirit.

The devil will give you one excuse after another for not spending time with God. Get serious with God and cry out to Him. *The Word of God and fellowship with Him will change you.* Paul says in Philippians 4:13, "I can do all things through Christ which strengtheneth me" (KJV). In other words, there is nothing in all creation you can't do through the power of Jesus Christ.

Use the problems that come against you as opportunities to grow. Find out what God will do because He loves you! If you will lean on God and let God love you and you love Him, you can forget all the trying to operate in faith and enter into rest.

❧

All blessings will come through letting God love you.

GOD'S WORD FOR YOU

But God shows and clearly proves His [own] love for us by the fact that while we were still sinners, Christ (the Messiah, the Anointed One) died for us.

ROMANS 5:8

Love Is Unconditional

According to God's Word, He loved us before the world was formed, before we loved Him or believed in Him or had ever done anything either good or evil.

God does not require us to earn His love, and we must not require others to earn ours. We must realize that love is something we are to become. It is not something we do and then don't do. We cannot turn it on and off, depending on who we want to give it to and how they are treating us.

As believers in Jesus Christ, the love we are to manifest to the world is the unconditional *love of God* flowing through us to them. We cannot understand this God-kind of love with our minds. It far surpasses mere knowledge. It is a revelation that God gives to His children by the Holy Spirit.

Unconditional love thinks long range. It sees what people can become if only someone will love them. That is what God did for us. He looked long range and saw that His unconditional love could conform us to the image of His Son.

Receive God's mercy and love; you cannot give away something you do not have.

GOD'S WORD FOR YOU

Do not let yourself be overcome by evil, but overcome (master) evil with good.

ROMANS 12:21

God's Love Overcomes and Transforms

A mean, evil individual can be completely transformed by regular, persistent doses of God's love. Because people's religious experiences in many cases have been unfulfilling to them, they have never entered into a relationship with Jesus Christ that is personal enough for them to begin receiving His healing, transforming love.

Religion often gives people rules to follow and laws to keep. It leads them to believe they must earn God's love and favor through good works. That is the exact opposite of true biblical teaching.

God's Word says that "mercy triumphs over judgment" (James 2:13 NKJV). God's goodness leads men to repentance (Romans 2:4), not the keeping of laws and rules. Jesus did not come to give man religion. He came to give man a deep personal love relationship with the Father through Him.

God's unconditional love does not allow people to remain the same; instead, it loves them while they are changing. Jesus said that He did not come for the well, but for the sick (Matthew 9:12). Our world today is sick, and there is no answer for what ails it except Jesus Christ and all that He stands for.

Unconditional love will overcome evil and transform lives.

GOD'S WORD FOR YOU

Love bears up under anything and everything that comes, is ever ready to believe the best of every person, its hopes are fadeless under all circumstances, and it endures everything [without weakening].

Love never fails [never fades out or becomes obsolete or comes to an end].

1 CORINTHIANS 13:7-8

*L*OVE NEVER FAILS

The God-kind of love bears up under anything and everything that comes. It endures everything without weakening. It is determined not to give up on even the hardest case. The hard-core individual who persists in being rebellious can be eventually melted by love. The Bible says, "While we were yet in weakness [powerless to help ourselves], at the fitting time Christ died for (in behalf of) the ungodly" (Romans 5:6).

It is hard to keep showing love to someone who never seems to appreciate it or even respond to it. It is difficult to keep showing love to those individuals who take from us all we are willing to give, but who never give anything back.

We are not responsible for how others act, only how we act. We have experienced the love of God by His mercy, and now He commands us to show that same kind of love to the world. Our reward does not come from man, but from God. Even when our good deeds seem to go unnoticed, God notices and promises to reward us openly for them: ". . . your deeds of charity may be in secret; and your Father Who sees in secret will reward you openly" (Matthew 6:4).

God is love, and love never quits.

GOD'S WORD FOR YOU

For out of His fullness (abundance) we have all received [all had a share and we were all supplied with] one grace after another and spiritual blessing upon spiritual blessing and even favor upon favor and gift [heaped] upon gift.

JOHN 1:16

BELIEVE AND RECEIVE GOD'S LOVE

Again and again, the Bible speaks of receiving from God. He is always pouring out His blessing, and we should, as empty, thirsty vessels, learn to take in freely all that He offers us.

In the spiritual realm, when you and I believe something, we receive it into our heart. In the world, we are taught to believe what we see. In God's Kingdom, we must learn to believe first, and then we will see manifested what we have believed (received, admitted in our heart).

When Jesus said that whatever we ask of God, believing, will be *granted* to us, He was saying that we will receive it *free*.

One of our biggest challenges is that we do not trust the word "free." We quickly find out in the world's system that things really are not free. Even when we are told they are free, there is usually a hidden cost somewhere.

But God's Kingdom of grace and love is not like the world's. God's wondrous love is a gift He freely gives us. All we need to do is open our hearts, believe His Word, and receive it with thankfulness.

Believe that God loves you with an everlasting love.

GOD'S WORD FOR YOU

And we know (understand, recognize, are conscious of, by observation and by experience) and believe (adhere to and put faith in and rely on) the love God cherishes for us. God is love, and he who dwells and continues in love dwells and continues in God, and God dwells and continues in him.

1 JOHN 4:16

*U*NDERSTAND GOD'S LOVE

First John 4:16 is a key scripture for me because it says that *we should be conscious and aware of God's love and put faith in it.* I was unconscious and unaware of God's love for a long time; therefore, I was not putting faith in His love for me.

When the Holy Spirit convicted me, I did not know how to say, "Yes, I made a mistake," then go to God, ask for His forgiveness, receive His love, and press on. Instead, I would spend hours and even days feeling guilty about each little thing I did wrong. I was literally tormented! John tells us that fear has torment, but that the perfect love of God casts out fear (1 John 4:18). God's love for me was perfect because it was based on Him, not on me. So even when I failed, He kept loving me.

God's love for you is perfect. When you fail, do you stop receiving God's love and start punishing yourself by feeling guilty and condemned? Don't listen to the devil's lie. Understand and believe God's intense love for you. Don't carry the enemy's burden of guilt. Believe and receive God's yoke of love.

God intends to love us.
He has to love us — He is love!

GOD'S WORD FOR YOU

. . . you are living the life of the Spirit, if the [Holy] Spirit of God [really] dwells within you [directs and controls you].

ROMANS 8:9

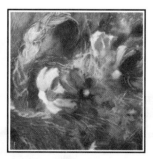

ℒET LOVE TAKE CHARGE

When love takes charge of us (which is another way of saying, when God takes charge of us), we cannot think bad things about people. We don't even want to.

We are not really living the life of the Spirit until we allow the Holy Spirit to control every area of our life. He will certainly never get control of our life until He has control of our thoughts and words.

Being led by the Spirit is central to a victorious Christian life. As long as we think our own thoughts and speak our own words, we will never experience victory.

Our life is a reflection of our thoughts. It is impossible to have a good life unless we have trained ourselves to have good thoughts. If we want others to see Jesus reflected in our life, then His mind must be reflected in us. We must be led by the Spirit in our thinking; that is where all Spirit-led living begins.

Be determined to love God, yourself, and others with your thoughts. Let God's love take charge in your life.

We can let the mind of the flesh control us, or we can choose the Holy Spirit and His way of thinking.

LOVING
OTHERS

*Love is a divine circle.
First, God loves us, and by faith
we receive His love. We then love
ourselves in a balanced way. We give
love back to God, and then we
learn to love other people.*

GOD'S WORD FOR YOU

By this shall all [men] know that you are My disciples, if you love one another [if you keep on showing love among yourselves].

JOHN 13:35

six

LOVING OTHERS

 t took me about forty-five years to realize that love was not the main focus in my life. We need to show the world Jesus. We do that by walking in His love.

Jesus Himself taught on love and walked in love. The world is looking for love, and God is love (1 John 4:8). God wants Christians who are committed to developing the character of Jesus Christ in their own lives and then go out as Christ's ambassadors (2 Corinthians 5:20).

To be His ambassadors, we must have our minds renewed to what love really is. Love is not a feeling we have; it is a decision to treat people the way Jesus would treat them.

When we truly commit to walk in love, it usually causes a huge shift in our lifestyle. Many of our ways—our thoughts, our conversation, our habits— have to change. Love is tangible; it is evident to everyone who comes in contact with it.

Loving others does not come easily or without personal sacrifice. Each time we choose to love someone, it will cost us something—time, money, or effort. That's why we are told to count the cost before we make the commitment (Luke 14:25-33).

Loving others does not depend on our feelings;
it's a choice me make.

GOD'S WORD FOR YOU

They tie up heavy loads, hard to bear, and place them on men's shoulders, but they themselves will not lift a finger to help bear them.

MATTHEW 23:4

TAKE THE PRESSURE OFF OTHER PEOPLE

You and I pressure ourselves and other people when we have unrealistic expectations. God does not want us to live under this kind of pressure.

We can expect more out of people than they are able to give us. Continued pressure on people we are in relationship with will ultimately cause the collapse of that relationship. *All people everywhere are looking for love and acceptance.*

I remember the years I furiously tried to change my husband, Dave, and each of our children in different ways. Those were frustrating years, because no matter what I tried, it didn't work!

As humans, all of us require space, or freedom, to be who we are. We want to be accepted as we are. We don't want people giving us the message, even subtly, that we must change in order to be "in."

I am not saying that we must accept sin in other people and merely put up with it. I am saying that *the way to change is prayer, not pressure!* If we love people and pray for them, God will work.

For change to last, it must come from the inside out. Only God can cause that type of heart change.

❧

We cannot change people by pressuring them or by nagging them. Only prayer and God's love will work.

GOD'S WORD FOR YOU

But if anyone has this world's goods (resources for sustaining life) and sees his brother and fellow believer in need, yet closes his heart of compassion against him, how can the love of God live and remain in him?

Little children, let us not love [merely] in theory or in speech but in deed and in truth (in practice and in sincerity).

1 JOHN 3:17-18

*L*OVING WITH MATERIAL GOODS

Many people love things and use people to get them. God intends for us to love people and use things to bless them. Sharing our possessions with others is one way to move love from the "talking-about-it stage" to the "doing-it stage."

God has given us a heart of compassion, but by our own choice we open or close it. As believers in Jesus Christ, God gives us His Spirit and puts a new heart in us. Ezekiel 11:19 says that this new heart is sensitive to God's touch. Something deep in every believer wants to help others. However, selfishness can make us so aggressive about our own desires that we become oblivious to the needs around us.

People are hurting everywhere. Some are poor; others are sick or lonely. Still others are emotionally wounded or have spiritual needs. A simple act of kindness to an insecure person can make that individual feel loved and valuable.

People can get caught in the trap of striving to have more. The struggle often produces little or no results. We should strive to excel in giving to others. If we do so, we will find that God makes sure we have enough to meet our own needs plus plenty to give away.

*There is no greater blessing
than giving to others in need.*

GOD'S WORD FOR YOU

As it is written, He [the benevolent person] scatters abroad; He gives to the poor; His deeds of justice and goodness and kindness and benevolence will go on and endure forever!

2 CORINTHIANS 9:9

Everyone Needs a Blessing

It is both good and scriptural to bless the poor. They should be one of our primary targets.

Look for people who are needy and bless them. Share what you have with those who are less fortunate than you are. But remember, everyone needs a blessing—even the rich, the successful, and those who appear to have everything.

We all need to be encouraged, edified, complimented, and appreciated. We all get weary at times and need other people to say to us, "I just wanted to let you know that I appreciate you and all you do."

I believe God blesses us so we can be a blessing —not only in a few places, but everywhere we go! So remember to sow into the poor and the rich, the downtrodden and the successful (2 Corinthians 9:6-7).

If you live to meet needs and to bring others joy, you will find "joy unspeakable" in the process (1 Peter 1:8 KJV).

I want to leave something as a result of my journey through life. I refuse to pass through it as a "taker." I have decided to be a "giver." I want to bless people in tangible ways. I pray that you have the same desire.

*Start using what you have to be a blessing,
and your well will never run dry.*

GOD'S WORD FOR YOU

Love one another with brotherly affection [as members of one family], giving precedence and showing honor to one another.

ROMANS 12:10

LOVE GIVES PREFERENCE TO OTHERS

Giving preference to others requires a willingness to adapt and adjust. It means to allow others to go first or to have the best of something. Each time we show preference, we have to make a mental adjustment. We were planning to be first, but we decide to be second. We are in a hurry, but we decide to wait on someone else who seems to have a greater need.

A person is not yet rooted and grounded in love until he or she has learned to show preference to others (Ephesians 3:17 NKJV). Anyone who wants to be a leader in the Kingdom of God must be willing to be a servant (Matthew 23:11).

We have multiple opportunities to adapt and adjust almost every day. If we are locked into our plans, we will have a difficult time doing so. Don't just learn to adjust, but learn to do it with a good attitude. Learning to do these things is learning to walk in love and humility.

Jesus humbled Himself and came to the earth as the Son of Man to save us. We cannot show preference and help others unless we are willing to follow His example and humble ourselves.

Only the Holy Spirit can change us from proud individuals into humble servants of God and man.

117

GOD'S WORD FOR YOU

And Peter opened his mouth and said: Most certainly and thoroughly I now perceive and understand that God shows no partiality and is no respecter of persons.

ACTS 10:34

ℒOVE IS IMPARTIAL

If love is unconditional, then it must not show partiality.

This does not mean that we cannot have special friends or that we cannot be more involved with certain people. It means that we cannot treat some people one way and other people a different way. Our love is not unconditional if we are only kind to those with whom we are good friends, and not care how we treat those who are of no interest or importance to us.

God has given me several special friends in my life who are "in the same flow" as I am. But He has also taught me to treat everyone with respect, to make them feel valued, to listen to them when they are talking to me and not to judge them in a critical way.

Our love walk can readily be seen by how we treat people who cannot do us any good, people with whom we are not interested in developing a relationship. Loving others frequently requires sacrifice. It requires that we put others first, doing what benefits them, and not just us.

The Word of God tells us that He does not show partiality, that He is no respecter of persons. As His representatives, we also are not to show partiality or practice favoritism.

*Let God show you how to love
everyone without partiality.*

GOD'S WORD FOR YOU

For you, brethren, were [indeed] called to freedom; only [do not let your] freedom be an incentive to your flesh and an opportunity or excuse [for selfishness], but through love you should serve one another.

For the whole Law [concerning human relationships] is complied with in the one precept, You shall love your neighbor as [you do] yourself.

GALATIANS 5:13-14

*F*REE TO BE SERVANTS

Jesus said, in essence, "If you love Me, you will obey Me" (John 14:21). To say "I love Jesus" and walk in disobedience is deception. Words are wonderful, but a full love walk must be much more than words.

I definitely love my husband, but the fulfillment of love must find some service to flow through. How can I say I love my husband if I never want to do anything for him? It is very easy to slide into the worldly flow of "everybody wait on me," but I am determined to swim upstream, against the pull of my flesh, and to be a servant and a blessing everywhere I go.

Jesus instructed His disciples to feed the hungry, give water to the thirsty, clothe the naked, care for the sick, and visit those in prison (Matthew 25:34-45). Jesus makes it very plain that if we have done nothing kind for others, then we have done nothing for Him.

Serving others sets them free to love. It disarms even the most hateful individual. The whole purpose in being a servant is to show others the love of God that He has shown us so that they too can share in it—and then pass it on.

When we serve others in love, God will reward us with a sense of His manifest Presence.

GOD'S WORD FOR YOU

For though we walk (live) in the flesh, we are not carrying on our warfare according to the flesh and using mere human weapons.

For the weapons of our warfare are not physical [weapons of flesh and blood], but they are mighty before God for the overthrow and destruction of strongholds,

[Inasmuch as we] refute arguments and theories and reasonings and every proud and lofty thing that sets itself up against the [true] knowledge of God; and we lead every thought and purpose away captive into the obedience of Christ (the Messiah, the Anointed One).

2 CORINTHIANS 10:3-5

DON'T LET SELFISHNESS WIN THE WAR

We are definitely in a war. The Bible teaches us that the weapons of our warfare are not carnal, natural weapons, but ones that are mighty through God for the pulling down of strongholds. The stronghold of love grown cold must be pulled down in our lives.

I believe Satan has launched high-tech spiritual warfare against the church, using humanism, materialism, and widespread selfishness as his bait. We must win the war against these things, and the only way to combat them is with a strong love walk.

Purposely forgetting about ourselves and our problems and doing something for someone else while we are hurting is one of the most powerful things we can do to overcome evil.

When Jesus was on the cross in intense suffering, He took time to comfort the thief next to Him (Luke 23:39-43). When Stephen was being stoned, he prayed for those stoning him, asking God not to lay the sin to their charge (Acts 7:59-60).

If the church of Jesus Christ, His body here on earth, will wage war against selfishness and walk in love, the world will begin to take notice.

Walking in love is spiritual warfare.

GOD'S WORD FOR YOU

And let us consider and give attentive, continuous care to watching over one another, studying how we may stir up (stimulate and incite) to love and helpful deeds and noble activities.

HEBREWS 10:24

Pleasant words are as a honeycomb, sweet to the mind and healing to the body.

PROVERBS 16:24

DEVELOP THE HABIT OF LOVE

If we intend to develop the habit of love, then we must develop the habit of loving people with our words. Multitudes of people need someone to believe in them. They have been wounded by wrong words, but right words can bring healing in their lives.

The fleshly (lower, sensual) nature points out flaws, weaknesses, and failures. It seems to feed on the negatives in life. It sees and magnifies all that is wrong with people and situations. But the Bible says in Romans 12:21 that we are to overcome evil with good.

Walking in the Spirit (continually following the prompting or leading, guiding, and working of the Holy Spirit through our own spirit instead of being led by our emotions) requires being positive. God is positive, and in order to walk with Him, we must agree with Him (Amos 3:3).

It is easy to find something wrong with everyone, but love covers a multitude of sins: "Above all things have intense and unfailing love for one another, for love covers a multitude of sins [forgives and disregards the offenses of others]" (1 Peter 4:8).

Believing the best of people and speaking words that build them up is one way of loving them.

THE HARRISON HOUSE VISION

*Proclaiming the truth and the power
Of the Gospel of Jesus Christ
With Excellence;*

*Challenging Christians to
Live victoriously,
Grow spiritually,
Know God intimately.*

JOYCE MEYER

Joyce Meyer has been teaching the Word of God since 1976 and in full-time ministry since 1980. Joyce's Life In The Word radio broadcasts are heard across the country, and her television broadcasts are seen around the world. She travels extensively, sharing her life-changing messages in Life In The Word conferences and in local churches.

Joyce and her husband, Dave, are the parents of four children. They make their home in St. Louis, Missouri.

Additional copies of this book are available from your local bookstore.

If this book has changed your life, we would like to hear from you.

Please write us at:

▣ Harrison House Publishers
P. O. Box 35035 • Tulsa, OK 74153
www.harrisonhouse.com

To contact the author, write:
Joyce Meyer Ministries
P. O. Box 655 • Fenton, Missouri 63026

or call: (636) 349-0303

Internet Address: www.joycemeyer.org

In Canada, write: Joyce Meyer Ministries Canada, Inc.
Lambeth Box 1300 • London, ON N6P 1T5

or call: (636) 349-0303

In Australia, write: Joyce Meyer Ministries-Australia
Locked Bag 77 • Mansfield Delivery Centre
Queensland 4122

or call: (07) 3349 1200

In England, write: Joyce Meyer Ministries
P. O. Box 1549 • Windsor • SL4 1GT
or call: 01753 831102